Couldn't keep it to myself

Yemaja Jubilee

Couldn't keep it to myself

Yemaja Jubilee

Jubilee, Yemaja

Couldn't Keep It To Myself

Copyright © 2018 by KWE Publishing LLC

Original manuscript copyright by Yemaja Jubilee

Editors: Belinda Todd, Deborah Woodard, Kimberley Eley, Merrijane Yerger, Rebekah Lynn Pierce

Artful illistrations by: Tina McGlynn, Faithe Norrell, Susan Moncure

Cover Artwork by: Tina McGlynn

Photography by: Robert Lee Sims III, Frank Anderson

ISBN (paperback) 978-0-9993620-6-8 – ISBN (ebook) 978-0-9993620-7-5
Library of Congress Control Number: 2017962952

Yemaja Jubilee
P.O. Box 12
Saxe, Va. 23967
(434) 808.2472
landnluv@aol.com

KWE
PUBLISHING

For all the women who have encircled my life

ACKNOWLEDGEMENTS

To my Beloved daughter, Cozzette Dushon Brown-Abrams, I thank you for choosing me as your earthly mother and your friend. You are the reason it was necessary for me to become a physically, emotionally and spiritually healthy human being.

To Merrijane Yerger and Kayelily Middleton, my oldest and dearest soul companions who took my hand and opened my heart to explore my internal terrain, helping me chart the course of these pages of my life.

To L. Roi Boyd III, thank you for sharing this earthly adventure with me. Sharing these poems with you changed the trajectory of my life and allowed my creative self to blossom. For this and so much more, my heart is eternally filled with gladness and gratitude.

To Belinda Todd, thank you for your continuous support and insightful edits that challenged my thought processes from the very beginning.

To Deborah Woodard, thank you for your edits on structure and spiritual guidance.

To Kimberley Eley, thank you for your positive attitude and keeping me on task and motivated. Your edits and technical assistance have allowed me to learn how this process works.

To Rebekah Lynn Pierce, thank you for your help in assisting me to "steer the course" through the terrain of punctuation, grammar, and fluidity of text.

To Tina McGlynn, thank you for your awesome and amazing art which brought tears to my eyes. The beauty and vibrant colors led me to see a portion of myself reflected in the art. Your work resonates deep in my soul.

To Joel Fletcher, thank you for all the hours you labored to bring the illustration ideas in my mind into manifestation.

To Faithe Norrell and Susan Moncure, thank you both for stepping in at the last minute to create art for this book.

To Rob Lee, thank for your professionalism and your photography and aesthetic sense that helped enhance the art in this book.

To Frank Anderson, thank you for always being there, your help in photographing the additional artwork for this project is greatly appreciated.

Most of all thanks to Merrijane Yerger, whose final critique and formatting of this work has accelerated it from a "raw", "rough-hewn" collection of poetry and stories to a mature volume of inspiration. Your contributions are greatly appreciated, more than you'll ever know.

Contents

INTRODUCTION

At age 15, I began writing in my diary about what was happening inside of me and my reactions to the world around me. My diary became the only safe place where I could express my feelings out loud to myself. It kept my secrets. The fear of my parents or anyone knowing me from the inside out was too risky and shameful.

My first entry was about getting it right. After faking my "come to Jesus moment" at one of the many churches we attended, I found I could only be honest in my diary. It was on those pure white pages that I submerged myself to cleanse my soul. It was there alone with God and my pen, that I felt free enough to admit I needed "to get right with the Lord."

My private musings turned into journaling, which soon began to include my aspirations, inspiration and longings. I expressed myself more and more through poetry. One of my first favorite memories that I wrote about was standing in the center of a circle of my girlfriends and cousins stretching my arms out and spinning around and around singing, "Little Sally Walker." It's a children's game that allowed each one of us the freedom to act out the words we were singing. "Little Sally Walker" was my first taste of a lyrical, poetic rhythm that has filled my life with poetry, dance and singing to this day. Unfortunately, "Little Sally Walker" would lead me astray through my "growing up" years.

I journaled and wrote poetry from age 16 to 39. Much to my dismay, I saved only one poem from those sexually formative years. In 1985, I began to write more and many of the poems I have selected for this book come from that period of my evolving self. This collection of poems details my inner transformation. They tell my story through relationships, addictions and crippling negative thinking. Most of all, they detail how I came to love myself and establish a deeply personal relationship with the Creator of the Universe, the *God of my understanding,* which I now call MOTHER LOVE BEAUTY – MY BELOVED.

Love and loved was what I felt every time my mother sang, whether at home or at church. One of my favorite songs that she loved to sing was **"I Said I Wasn't Gonna to Tell Nobody,"** by Reverend Alex Bradford. The chorus of this song became the golden thread woven through the tapestry of my life and my poetry. It goes like this:

You oughta been there
You oughta been there
When He saved my soul
Saved my soul
You oughta been there
You oughta been there
When He put my name on the Roll

You know that I
Started walkin'
And I

Started talkin'
Then I
Started singin'
Then I
Started shoutin'
What the Lord has done for me!

Chorus:
I said I wasn't gonna tell nobody,
But I couldn't keep it to myself!
Couldn't keep it to myself!
Couldn't keep it to myself!
I said I wasn't gonna tell nobody,
But I couldn't keep it to myself
What the Lord has done for me!

It is my desire that you will come to see as I did, that my struggles, pain, sorrows and depression allowed me to grow and become all that the Creator would have me to be. I am sharing my poems in hopes that they will inspire you to come to know that you, too, are a wonderfully and marvelously made spiritual being.

Little Sally Walker

Little Sally Walker,
Sitting in a saucer
Weeping and crying over a nice young man.

Rise, Sally, rise:
Wipe your weeping eyes.
Put your hands on your hip,
Let your back bone slip;
Shake it to the east, O baby,
Shake it to the west;
Shake it to the one you love the best.

Lawrence W. Levine, *Black Culture and Black Consciousness: Afro-American Folk Thought from Slavery to Freedom,* 2007 (p.198)

LITTLE DUCE ANN BROWN

From playing "Little Sally Walker," I created a new name for myself: Little Duce Ann Brown. When I was 16, I wrote the first poem about the community and the church deacons and deaconesses. Within yelling distance of my house was what was known as a "juke joint." On Friday and Saturday nights of every week, just as it was getting dark, the action started and lasted until the early morning hours. I was forbidden to go, of course. But I would look out from my bedroom window to watch what was happening. It was fascinating and exciting. The music, the cars, the loud voices all intrigued me. Even more intriguing were some of the church folk I saw coming and going. The followings words flowed through my confused teenaged mind like a rushing river and I asked questions like, "Where Have All the Christian Folk Gone?"

WHERE HAVE ALL THE CHRISTIAN FOLK GONE?

Where have all the Christian folk gone?
They sure ain't gone to no heavenly home.
Why Brother Joe, I saw you at Sister CeCe's last night
Coming out the back door pawing all over Bro Sam's wife!

Oh, by the way, Brother Sam, wait just a pea-picking minute
It was you I saw going to the Drakes Branch ABC store.
If the truth be told, you have become a regular customer.
And you been buying more and more.
I see you carrying larger brown bags than before!

Some of y'all be thinking Sister Sally
Been having Bible Study classes
At her house on Wednesday nights.
Why that's just a lie! A sin and a shame I tell you.
I'm willing to bet that's not all that was done in Jesus' name.

Brother Earl and I saw Reverend Shakey
And the highly-esteemed Reverend Likado shoving money
In Sister Sally's apron pocket
When they were coming out of her house.
They be laughing and saying all those dirty words

That I dare not repeat
Like "she sure knows how to make a man feel
The holy ghost from his head to his feet."
They'll be coming back every week.

Now Sister Mary Alice, her be known
As a shy fragile thing in the church social circle.
She was widowed very early in life
But the other church ladies been whispering behind her back
"That ain't right."
They be saying she be slipping and cocktail sipping
At the Manzel Bach, better known as the
Pink Pussy Haven in our neck of the woods.

Then some of y'all Deacons be sitting on the church pews
On Sunday morning and saying
"Well, well" from the amen corner
While the Sisters be singing "Lord have mercy on me!"
Where have all the Christian folk gone?
They sure ain't going to no heavenly home!

LITTLE DUCE ANN BROWN

Little Duce Ann, sitting in the sand,
Weeping and crying for a nice young man.
Rise, rise, wipe your eyes.
Turn to the East and turn to the West,
Turn to the one that you love best.
Put your hands on your hips, let your backbone slip!
Shake it to the East and shake it to the West!
Shake it to the man that you love best!
Now you and your man are worthy to stand life's test!

MRS. ANN DELORIS BROWN JOHNSON MCCARGO

Little Duce Ann became an adult. After two failed marriages (to Mr. Johnson for five years, Mr. McCargo for six months) and life as a single parent, I was wounded, very fragile and unsure of myself. I was not at that time willing to pay the higher cost of change. I was not even aware that I needed to change, for my "normal" way of behaving was the norm of everyone around me. I lingered and wallowed in the false belief that I needed to be rescued by a man. However, after moving to Tennessee with my live-in boyfriend at the time, I caught a glimpse of the possibility that the change was going to come. **TIME** was written about three weeks after I arrived in Tennessee.

TIME

The time has come
for positive changes
in my life.

The time has come
for negative thoughts
not to be part of my days.

The time has come
for me to dream,
visualize and capture

What my heart
Is yearning for,
What my heart
Is seeking after.

MRS. ANN DELORIS BROWN JOHNSON MCCARGO TUNSTALL

I now know that my need to be taken care of, my feelings of shame, guilt and my need to be accepted by my dad caused me to behave in unhealthy ways. I was a people pleaser, a caretaker, controlling and in denial about my role in my own unhappiness.

So, once again, I did what I had been conditioned to do: I got married again. After coming home with my boyfriend for Christmas, my father took him to the back bedroom and the very Reverend Mr. Brown gave him a sermon on the virtues of marriage rather than burning hell for "living in sin" with his daughter. My boyfriend proposed, and we were married the following summer by my father. This marriage to Mr. Tunstall lasted four years. There was a lot of journaling during this time. What happened to all those pages and poems I'll never know. I can't recall. Maybe they ended up in the ash heap during the fiery winter of my discontent.

It was after divorce number three from Mr. Tunstall that my inner journey began. I became willing to focus on myself. My feelings of low self-esteem, denial, unworthiness and using others and food to sedate the pain required that I surrender to a power greater than myself. Most of all, acceptance of myself, forgiving myself and loving myself were now at the forefront of my life. They had to be if I was to obtain any peace and inner serenity. I couldn't live another day feeling so lost and miserable, so alone with myself.

Yes, I was afraid! Yes, it was very dark times, and at one point, I wanted to end my life. Depressed and filled with shame, I reached out and sought help from a professional therapist. Finally, I was able, by the Grace of God, to make a commitment to myself and my teenage daughter to live and to keep on living no matter what.

This selection of poems illustrates in words my inner journey. Hopefully, they will inspire you no matter where you are on your journey and they will light the way for healing and self-care for you as well.

SHE

My mind was inspired today
By someone God sent my way.
She wore a beaming smile
I could tell her heart was filled with love.

As she began to talk and explain
I felt "Wow!"
This feels good
To be in the presence
Of positive thinking again.

As I began to share my hopes and ideas
Even my dreams
I felt completely at ease.
I knew when the conversation ended
She was someone

I would come to know and love her.
At last I was able to call her my friend
She was me and I was she.

INVITATION #1

Come join us at our home to fill it with joy, sweetness and laughter.

Come share and listen to the melodies of voices as they sing and chatter.

Come open your hearts, minds and perceptions to a new experience. Where old friends and friends who are yet to be ignore the sometimes-unspoken lines of color and cultural traditions.

Come to partake of a scrumptious, delicious and delightful bounty prepared especially for you with love as a potent elixir.

Come, come and be, to do a new thing during this period of joy and jubilation, to participate in a warm, fun-loving celebration,
A celebration of you and me.

WHAT DO I SEE?

When I look at me, I see no one's daughter, wife or mother.
When I look at me, I see no doormat or a sign on my back that says, 'walk on me.' When I look at me, I see no victim, one beaten down by the suffering of my own choices.

What do I see? Lordy have mercy, what do I see?

I see a warm and caring human being
I see a sensitive, sensual, sexy and spiritual person
I see a person who loves God and appreciates life's many gifts
I see brilliance, intelligence, creativity and grace
I see beauty that is continuously evolving from the inside out
I see a spiritual being, a breathing organism
I see a soul who wears a human suit that clothes her true divine identity.
I see the luminosity of Spirit glowing in me – Holy Oneness
I see the most precious gift of all that binds us together
I see you in me and me in you
Now run tell that!

SHITTY DAYS

Life is funny sometimes with its many twists and turns.
Life deals some days as sweet as the taste of honey on the tip of your tongue.
Then Life decides as if through no desire of your own, NO!
Today will be a shit day for you!
Moreover, life will dump stinking loads of shit on you to see exactly what you are made of.
However, you keep on going and striving for the highest good.
You allow yourself to smile and laugh right in the face of this shitty adversity.
How dare Life be so cruel and treat you this way!
You bow your head to your heart and utter a soulful prayer to the Source of the Universe who always, always has your back.
It replies in the quietude of your soul, your sanctuary,
"Hey, Girlfriend, this is earth school, where you keep on learning and loving, even on shitty days."
How else will you know that you are made by Love?

Shitty days give you the fortitude to enjoy life for what it is truly meant to be: to love, to serve, to be the best spiritual being you can be in all circumstances.
Now, you have your eyes wide open and the internal essence of your soul leads the way—pay attention.
Now, it has been made very clear, these shitty days were just the Creator's way to give you the fertilizer that you need to grow, to be transformed, transmuted and to transcend to a higher plane of living.

LOOK WITHIN YOURSELF

Before you find fault in your brothers and sisters,
Look within yourself.
Before you point a finger to accuse, to blame, or pass on generational shame,
Look within yourself.
Before you become self-righteous (because you think you have all the answers, you are never
wrong, yet you swear, taking the Lord's name in vain),
Look within yourself.
Before you set yourself up to be judge and jury,
Look within yourself.
Before you call your sisters and brothers dumb, stupid, a worthless piece of shit, a nigger, a coon,
a bitch, the devil, or muther fucka,
Look within yourself.
Just look within yourself and you will know yourself.
What you see around you reflects what's within you.
If you look within and know yourself for who you really are, a loving and compassionate being,
light and shadow, you will see that you are one within and without.

IF I HAD MY WAY

If I had my way today,
in your presence
I would be

I would walk into a room
you would embrace me
with your smile and I would feel
       deep
              sensual
                     warm
                            pleasure
                                all over me.

If I had my way today
in your presence
I would be
       caressing your face with a soft, gentle touch of my fingers and hands,
          looking deep into the windows of your soul.

If I had my way today
in your presence
I would be
       running my long, slender fingers through your curly black hair
          in the ecstasy of mutual pleasure.

If I had my way today
in your presence
I would be
       laying my head upon your hairy chest
          as you caress me gently in a warm, comforting, nurturing way.

If I had my way today
 in your presence
 I would be
    in that joy that comes from giving and receiving and sharing,
      we would explode in pure unadulterated gratification.
      If I had my way
       In your presence
         We would be One.

I BE MISSING YOU

I be missing the smile on your face and feel of your arms in a warm embrace. Yes, I do!

I be missing the sound of your deep husky, manly voice and laying my head upon your hairy, moist chest.

I be missing the sound of your robust laughter and the sweetness of your soft tones as you whisper loving words in my ear, "Girl keep your feet on the ground; this is not a dream, because I am right here, right now."

Yes, my God, I do!

I be missing being hugged, held tight, squeezed under the moonlight and lying next to you on a cold winter night.

I be missing the caring, the sharing and the listening with compassion and understanding of all my doubts, fears and worries about what tomorrow may bring.

Yes, my God, I do!

I be missing those times when we would stay in bed all day not caring about the time of day.

I be missing the tingling sensation from just the holding of your hand. And the gentle pressure of your mouth sweetly applied to each one of my giggling toes.

Yes, My God, I do!

Yes, I be missing you, my love, I be missing you oh so much, so won't you please drop me a line, pick up the phone, for any kind of contact will do if I hear from you. You turkey you!

Well, it really does not matter! Our relationship was not meant to be, so it is best that you and I not stay in touch because you are not good for me, nor I for you.

4

MRS. ANN DELORIS BROWN JOHNSON MCCARGO TUNSTALL JUBILEE

For years, I heard sermons that made me feel worthless and ashamed. It was poison to my soul! Each week, I overdosed on the homiletic energy swirling 'round about me, sinking deeper into self-condemnation. I was stuck in the muck and mire of negative thinking. I believed God sat on a throne recording everything that I did. Further, the devil was responsible for my negative thoughts and behaviors. And I couldn't get away from either one. This lead to depression and I developed an eating disorder.

My therapist at the time sent me to a Twelve Step program, Overeater's Anonymous, which is based on Alcoholics Anonymous. With a sponsor, I began applying the Twelve Steps and Twelve Traditions of recovery to my life. I decided it was time to let go of the old limiting beliefs and behaviors.

That meant I could now replace my old concept of God with a concept of the Divine that worked in and for me. I wrote in my journal everything I needed God to be: loving, kind, compassionate and non-judgmental. I needed a God that accepted me as I am. Every day I affirmed: I love myself! I believe in myself! I value myself! God loves me and accepts me just as I am! I am a Beautiful, Black woman with so much to share! Often, I sat in a rocking chair and imagined that I was holding a baby in my lap, and I told the baby how wonderful she was. That baby was me!

As I grew into new ways of thinking about God, I was no longer willing to be subjected to shame and damnation. Slowly, I stopped attending any kind of church or religious activity that produced feelings of shame and conformity. When I did, I gave myself permission to leave. During this time of studying the Twelve Steps, a friend suggested I try Unity Church. So along with attending classes and making new friends, my self-worth increased. I felt loved and accepted for the first time at Unity.

I began to fill up with gratitude. These poems were written during this time.

THANK YOU!

Source, Benefactor, everlasting Father, I thank you for waking me up to see a new day dawning.

Divine Mother, giver of life, I thank you for the smell of the fresh spring air that I now breathe.

Protector, I thank you for sending Archangel Michael to watch over me as I slumbered peacefully through the night.

I AM, I thank you for the sounds of the blue birds and red birds singing their songs in the magnolia trees outside my bedroom window.

Allah, I thank you for the warmth of golden sunrays that give me warmth on a cold and damp winter afternoon.

Yahweh, I thank you for the sensations of the ground as my bare feet stroll through wet grass.

God, I thank you for my blood relatives and my new family of choice.

Shiva, I thank you for new friends and for old friends both far and near.

Atman, I thank you for opening my heart, clearing my mind, changing my perceptions, and allowing Mahatma's love to flow freely through me.

Love Beauty, Thank you! All the praises and my gratefulness are the highest form of praise that I know to give to you.

So, I now thank you for keeping me, showing me the way and always being there for me even when I had chosen another path. For now, I know that you are Love, you are Life and you are Truth. I am made in Love, by Love, for Love. For this and all aspects of myself, I am grateful!

CREATOR OF THIS DAY

Creator of this day, help me to live this wonderful, glorious new day according to your will and Divine plan.

Creator of this day, help me to live this **Magnificent Monday** by being kind, loving, and considerate to all humans, no matter their race or color, their need or creed.

Creator of this day, help me to live this **Triumphant Tuesday** being affectionate and compassionate to all who hold a special place in my heart.

Creator of this day, help me to live this **Wonderful Wednesday** being non-judgmental in my thinking, in my words and in accepting of other's faults and shortcomings as well as my own.

Creator of this day, help me to live this **Tranquil Thursday** by not being self-righteous toward others who choose not to live according to the Gospel of Ann Deloris Brown Johnson McCargo Tunstall.

Creator of this day, help me to live this **Fabulous Friday** being joyful and embracing the sweetness of your spirit, diving deeper into your well of goodness and mercy, which allows the flow of peace in my soul.

Creator of this day, help me to live this **Sweet Sassy Saturday** with dancing in my feet, savoring and moving to the rhythms and beats that vibrate and cause me to gyrate in the natural flow of Life.

Creator of this day, help me to live my life, knowing that I am always growing, never shaming or blaming others for the choices that were of my own making.

Creator of this day, help me to live my life trusting YOU, knowing you more and more each day, thanking you, mastering life's lessons, one by one.

Creator of this day, help me to live every day of my life knowing that every day is sacred, everything is holy and each day is to be lived like it is **Soul-Filled Sunday**.

ONENESS

I now walk in the light with great excitement and boldness because I am centered in the Divine who gives me wholeness.

Bigger, larger and greater than my mind can conceive, the Divine supplies all my daily needs.

So, I give praise and thanksgiving with a mighty roar 'cause with the Divine there is no such thing as a closed door.

I give my whole soul to the Spirit of peace and love pours down like a gentle spring shower from above.

I sup at the table of the Divine who feeds my hunger with sheer joy and sweet serenity.
No longer do I feel scattered and fragmented, worn or haggard.

I have found what my soul has been looking for—Oneness. I am connected, whole, to the source and giver of all Life, Love, Beauty -- GOD!

SISTERS SITTING IN THE BLESSINGS

We are *Sisters* sitting in the blessings all around us in this space and in this place right now.

Sisters proud to be who we are, aware of our struggles that have brought us to this very moment.

Sisters who are mindful of those who have walked this path before us. Our moms, grandmothers, aunts and cousins who made their own way, that we might reap the benefits of their struggles and sufferings.

Miss Leanne Davis, Aunt Fleeta Overton, my Mother, Marie Harris Brown, and a host of others who taught us children at their knees, and from their knees, sharing the prayers and the lessons they had learned.

Sisters who have been willing to uncover, discover and heal the darkness, the pain, grief, and sorrow from every nook and cranny in our souls, so that the truth can unfold, willingly told and we can be joyful and whole.

Sisters who refused to be beat up, told to sit down and shut up now. We refuse to allow anything to hold us back and be put down by guilt and shame, not ever again!

Sisters who recognize those that would harm her, defame her to keep her from her Divine inheritance of an abundant Life.

Sisters who are educated, motivated and each brimming with their own brilliance. And each knowing there is no need to tear one another down because each of us is blessed with different gifts and talents, and so together we all can shout halleluiah and dance around.

Sisters who can support each other through each rite of passage:
Moon cycles, birth cycles, growth cycles, wisdom cycles, death cycles—hell, even hetero-cycles, homo-cycles and bicycles rolling together through this thing called Life.

Sisters coming together in circles all around the world to hold each other's hands, sit in silence to heal the scars and wounds that are not always visible to the naked eye.

Sisters who once they healed themselves, acted as midwives to others to be by their sides so they can learn to do the same, and aid the release of trouble and deep seeded pain.

Sisters who are not ashamed of who they are, where they have been and share how they are not their stories, but keenly aware now of where we all are going.

Sisters who know that life is what you make of it and like a dance, life can teach you its flow, merging with the beats and rhythms, there is a peaceful hum produced by the soul.

Sisters who can dance, celebrate and appreciate all the grace, mercy, bounty and blessings which the Creator has so graciously bestowed upon us individually and collectively.

We then declare ourselves to be and always have been, ***Sisters sitting in the Blessing***. And so, it is!

5

YEMAJA

There was a time during these years when I began to sense that I was close to giving birth to my true self. I could feel the inner transformation occurring more and more each day. I was my own "doula" midwifing my own birthing, my own coming out. I had been through the dark contractions of my past. Those years were left behind. This lovely, laborious adventure has been giving birth to my own Divine Self, my True Self. Here I come. Here I am.

ON A HOLIDAY BY THE SEA

Dear One,

I am on a holiday by the sea, the roaring surf rushes to shore to plant its welcoming, salty kisses upon my cheek. I am honored by my sometime forgotten spirit and my wounded, weary soul has arisen again, refreshed, renewed, born again.

By the sea, by the sea, I surrendered all my worries, troubles and heavy woes to a loving, kind, merciful and gentle power; MOTHER LOVE BEAUTY cradled my heart and filled me with her joyous waves washing the seaweeds from the shore.

On a holiday by the sea, I willingly let go of arrogance, pride and self-centered ego with the ebb and flow of the morning tide. The sweetness of Love revitalized, refreshed and restored me to my **true divinity.**

On a holiday by the sea, as I hugged and held CeCe, my favorite rag doll, in a warm embrace, I connected with the child within. And I declared: "Little Duce Ann, where have you been? It is so good to know you once again. My, how you have changed"

At times, I have put Little Duce Ann up on a shelf in my mind. Forgetting her passion, joy, enthusiasm and love for life, turning circles, singing about her friend Sally Ann. In a soft, gentle and compassionate voice, she reminds me of her presence. Little Duce Ann shed light on all the darkness which used to reside in my soul. It's all gone today.

On a holiday by the sea, by the sea, I uncovered and discovered me. The Isness of Spirit and I Am that I Am--beautiful, beloved daughter of the Most High. My soul no longer cries out for me. Solitude has brought quietude and the sweet stillness of serenity has become my constant friend. And so, it is. That circle of life turning, turning, turning.

Wish you were here,

Love, Yemaja

TODAY

Tomorrow is not promised to us all, so we must live each moment of the day as it is given.

Today in my heart, I feel the deepening of my love and sobering longing to have you closer.

Today in my heart, I feel a desire to tell you how much I missed knowing you each passing moment.

Today in my heart, I feel I must let you know, your warmth, your caring and understanding are so appreciated.

Today in my heart, with gladness and lightness of spirit, I thank you for all the sweet golden moments that we share moment to moment.

Today in my heart, I feel desire, a fire in my soul, and so it must be told, this love affair that I now have with you surpasses all understanding. My heart is dancing!

Today in my heart, I can rest assured that I will have many more tomorrows with you 'cause my today will slowly become tomorrows and I will be blessed with togetherness and oneness by being connected to you…MOTHER LOVE BEAUTY.

DETOUR—NEW YORK CITY!
I FELL FOR THE LINE ONE MORE TIME! WARNING! THIS IS A TEST!
Looking back over these words, I clearly had not developed my newfound Self. This wedding and marriage, my last, proved to be nothing more than a feeble visitation from the old habit of "Hey, baby! You stroke my ego and I'll stroke yours." INVITATION #2 was further proof of my backsliding, delusional, ego-centric self, striving to be heard—still. This was the last vestige of the habituated self I had been learning to break free from. I couldn't stand it any longer. Trust me, it takes hard work, determination and great courage. To be free! And I'm still standing here today to tell about it. I am "woke!"

TOMORROW IS OUR WEDDING DAY

Tomorrow is our wedding day!
No shame, no guilt, no doubt or any fear as our day approaches, and our very sacred predestined moment draws very near.

Tomorrow is our wedding day!
No regrets, no remorse, no negative thoughts, not even any shoulds, woulds, or coulds.

Tomorrow is our wedding day!
In my sacred cherished self, I choose to ignore what others think, say or how they feel. For deep in my heart, I know the love I feel for you is very real.

Tomorrow is our wedding day!
It has been written, "All the whole world's a stage and all the men and women merely players," but I choose to believe that Divine order blessed, sanctified and ordained our union from the start.

Tomorrow is our wedding day!
When the stage is set, and the curtain goes up, all eyes will be upon us. It is our ceremony and our commitment to each other. It is neither an act nor an insignificant sideshow, or is it?

And even if there is no applause, no hip, hip hurray, no fanfare of any type, no congratulations, we will be filled with joy, ecstasy, happiness and great jubilation!

Tomorrow is our wedding day!
Yes, it is true, Love Beauty has not promised tomorrow to us all.
I will trust that we will be awakened by the Creator, Author of this Universe, and be blessed to see our wedding day. Then, my today would have become tomorrow, and I will be blessed to spend many more tomorrows with you.

INVITATION #2

Come grow with me, so you and I can be all that LOVE BEAUTY desires us to be.

So that you and I can soar high in the blue skies of life like mighty magnificent eagles.

So that you and I can walk hand in hand on this earthly journey and this emerging holographic adventure.

So that you and I can unite our spirits, open our hearts, evolve our minds and nurture our souls in a Cosmic Union.

So that you and I can hook a ride to the center of the Universe to the sound of the Divine's heartbeat at the intersection of you and me.

Come grow with me, dear heart, for we were never meant to be or do this alone, but to just remember we have always been a Divine spark of Light sent to shine, shine, shine.

NOT ANYMORE!

Ain't no slave who can be brow beaten, shackled with chains, head bowed down in shame and sold to the highest bidder. Not anymore!

Ain't no wench, who the master can rape, continuously sexually violate, birth his babies, which he then denies or never claims. Then we live with generational shame. Not anymore!

Ain't no nigger, nigra, nigress, or Negro who, because my skin is black, you hate, but let me turn my back, you imitate. Not anymore!

Ain't no colored person who must ride at the back of the bus and enter public places through the back door. Not anymore!

Ain't no mammy, nanny, or a maid who say, "yes ma'am" and makes your beds, cleans your filth, nurses your babies, raises your children, and mops your floors. Not anymore!

Ain't no cook who fries the chicken, bakes tarts and pies of all sorts. Then, with my Black, calloused, rough, ashy hands, I knead your bread, putting a part of my soul in every turn of the dough. Then you eat it, devouring a bit of my anger, shame and hate in every morsel and crumb. Not anymore!

Ain't no bitch with big tits, a hole in the middle of my thighs and big hind parts, which is a part of my God-given natural beauty, but used in many forms of sexual exploitation. Not anymore!

Ain't no mistress who waits for you, sitting by the phone while you are with your wife and I be at your beckoning call. Not anymore!

Ain't no slut who screws around with you, your friends or anyone who has a penis, be it for money or glory. I will not sell my soul even if it is to satisfy Tyrone, Butchy or Leroy. Not anymore!

Ain't no skizzer, hussy nor tramp, no arm candy for some old dog or high-tailed alley cat. Not anymore!

I done crossed over that river for the last time.

Spiritual

Spiritual Being

Spiritual Being Human

Spiritual Being Human Being

Spiritual Being Human Being Woman

Spiritual Being Human Being Woman of Colors

Soul Sister, Sister Girl, Girlfriend, Genuine, Authentic,

Compassionate, Caring, Warm, Loving, Generous, Kind, Forgiving,

Friend Spiritual, Sensual, Sensitive! I radiate beauty from the Inner Divine

essence of my soul, from the top of my head to the tip of my pinkie toes, I'm living

my life from inside out!

THE DANCE OF THE SSS GIRLS, Steps on Becoming Spiritual, Sensual, Sassy

Hey, Sister Girl! Do you or would you like to be an SSS girl?

An SSS girl has no shame, no inhibitions and does not believe in superstition!

An SSS girl remembers what her grandmother told her, "Why girl, you can catch more flies with honey than you can with vinegar."

An SSS girl shouts hip, hip, hooray for herself and others 'cause she knows from the inside out that life is great, life is grand and on the solid rock we stand.

An SSS girl knows her place in the world is not to be what you would have her to be!

An SSS girl knows in her, through her, as her, there ain't nothing else left for her to be but heavenly 'cause, girl, she is one of a kind.

An SSS girl knows her value, her own worth and why she was put on this earth! Guess what? It is not based on a Gucci bag, a Yves Saint Laurent dress, nor a pair of Jimmy Choo shoes.

An SSS girl does not live her life based upon shoulda, woulda, coulda, and by no means oughta. Girl, she has no regrets! Now run tell that!

An SSS girl lifts her hands in loud applause and high jubilation 'cause she knows without a doubt, from the inside out, she walks by faith, sowing fertile seeds of sweet serenity.

An SSS girl allows only sweet, soulful and loving words to flow from her lips and out of her mouth. She has no time for gossip, criticism, judgment and tales of woe, honey!

An SSS girl sings no victim song; she is too busy loving herself and others, living one day at a time, learning new things and knowing where her soul belongs. She is whole, a sacred being, not based in having a whole lot of money. Money ain't got nothing to do with it!

An SSS girl has no worries, no fears; sorrows no longer flood her soul. And even when the pains of everyday living run deep, she lets go and just surrenders all her self-doubt! She keeps her enemies at bay by praying for them and never cussing them out or going zip, zip, zip with her hands on her hips.

Hey, Sister Girl! Let's dance the dance together to the tune of the spiritual, sensual, sassy notes, tickling out our song on the keyboard of our lives!

6

WHAT'S IN A NAME?

What's your Name?
Pudding and Tane,
Ask me again and I will tell you the same.

Where do you live?
Down the lane.
What's your Number?
Cucumber.

What's your name?
It is not Jessie or Jane
Ask me again 'cause it'll never be the same.

Where do you live?
Under the purple umbrella
What's your number?
Cinderella.

Ann

Ann Deloris

Ann Deloris Brown

Ann Deloris Brown Johnson

Ann Deloris Brown Johnson McCargo

Ann Deloris Brown Johnson McCargo Tunstall

Ann Deloris Brown Johnson McCargo Tunstall Jubilee

Ann Deloris Brown, the name given to me on the day of my birth weighted down with shame, guilt and feelings of low self-worth. Sometimes I felt like the scum of the earth.

Worked hard every day of the week and spent all day Sunday going to church to save my sinful soul. The Sabbath day to me was never sacred or holy just an empty hole.

At age twenty-three, I married and became Ann Deloris Brown Johnson. Waited on my husband hand and foot, was the best lay he ever had, and we never lived happily ever after. No time for gaiety, fun, only room for my soul to feel sad.

That marriage, naturally crumble after all it was a house built on sand. I eagerly replaced Mrs. Johnson with Mrs. McCargo. Beat up, told to shut up and sit your ass down! "Second verse, same as the first", more misery and emotional pain, I felt like II might go insane.!
Name, Name, never a name of my own. Once again, let me drop this name, now I know I won't e a token to be played in a in a man's game--, or so I thought. so, I decide to choose the "things" instead of the name of a mane to fill the hole in my soul.

Name, Name, name number three, being alone was not for me because I had to be Ann Deloris Brown Johnson McCargo Tunstall. Fur coats, new cars, diamond watches and rings. My world was filled with a false sense, of self based upon material things. Drinking, snorting and smoking drugs of all kinds. Girl, this blew my mind and turned my world upside down. So, I sought solace in the name of the Lord to give me comfort and set me free one more time.

Name, Name, never a name of my own! Let's drop all these names. Now is the time to just let go of all this insanity, troubles and process this pain. Twelve Step groups of many different names gave me the courage to uncover and discover my true name.

Like the mystery of the butterfly, my life was transformed, no longer living in the dark, I come forth. I witnessed the beauty and magnificence of my soul being born again. I became a new being filled with the color of the rainbow surrounded by God's light.

Then on a warm summer night, in a lucid dream, all adorned within a shiny, golden necklace and a long flowing purple robe from my head to my toe, I saw myself lying on an alabaster alter. Hints of burning sage and lavender permeated the air, and out of nowhere, one by one, these Wise-Soul-Beings appeared, all dressed in white. Not a word was spoken as they all gathered around, chanting, praying and telepathically communicating, in a language only my heart could understand.

In unison, they all proclaimed and declared:
"YEMAJA, YEMAJA, YEMAJA"
Is now your name.

A name of your own, freely given, freely bestowed
"YEMAJA, YEMAJA, YEMAJA."

What's my name? What's my name?
"YEMJA, YEMAJA, YEMAJA!"

What's in a name?
Oneness. Wholeness.
Light, Love. Positivity.
No more shame, no need for game.
I am no longer the same.
I AM YEMAJA!

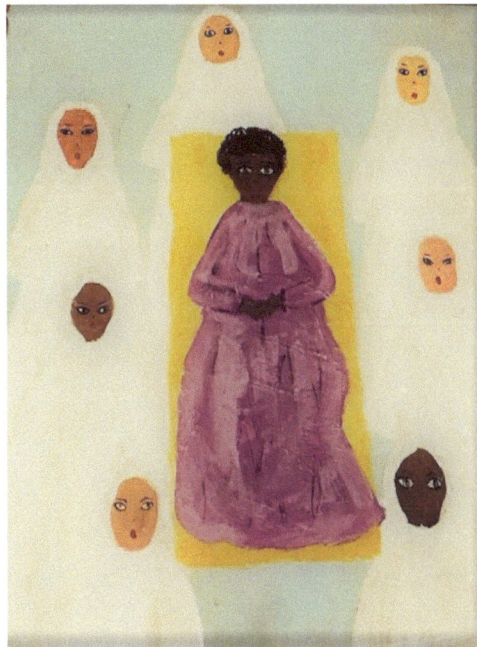

Not the end!

My Maternal Grandmother
Violet Harris, who was the
first woman I heard
pray in church.

My Paternal Grandmother
Lena Green Brown, who ruled with a
black iron skillet, and made dandelion
and blackberry wine.

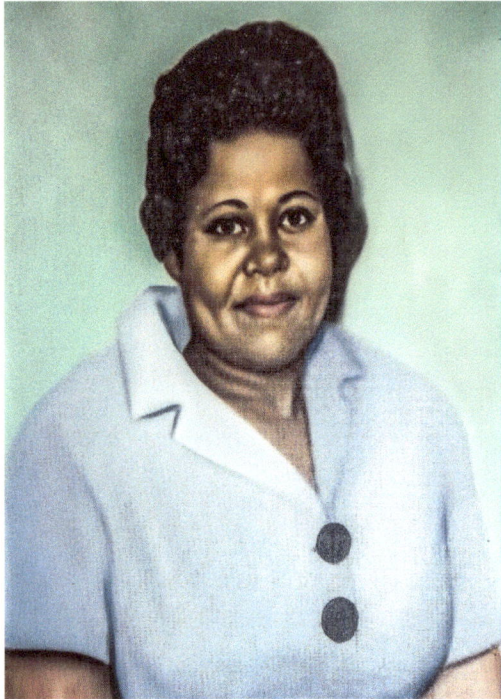

With Highest Regard, My Mother
Marie Harris Brown, who taught me to make
a meal out of nothing, her holy dance and
to love everybody

My Adoptive Mother
Arnette Wallington, who claimed me as
her daughter, after the death of my
mother and gave me a soft place to
grieve.

Cozzette DuShon Abrams
My lovely and beautiful daughter who also is my friend, my conscious at times, and one of my biggest supporters of me being all that I can be as well as a soft place for her when sorrows flood her soul.

INDEX OF POEMS

About the Author

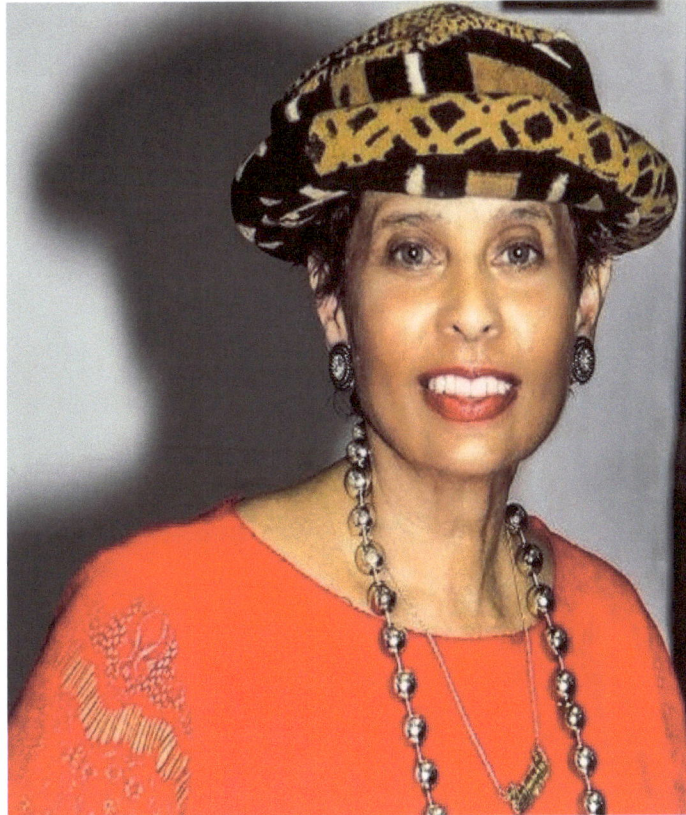

Yemaja Jubilee is a Life Coach, poet, Motivational/Inspirational Speaker, Workshop Facilitator and song writer. She is Co-Founding Director of Cultural Libations, a multidisciplinary arts and humanities company. Yemaja has co-produced the movie ***Black Wall Street: The Money, The Music and The People***, with RLP production, in addition to co-writing the theme song for the movie. She produces and hosts her own TV show, Love, Light and Positivity on Comcast TV of Richmond, Virginia, *(RVA).* She also serves as Creative Consultant for several other shows on Comcast TV.

Yemaja is a native of Charlotte County, Saxe, Virginia. Yemaja is a lover of trees and long walks. She is a lover of life and the belief that each day is a good day to be alive. She fills her days with joy, gratitude, and adventure. Her adventures spiritually and physical continue to allow, continue to allow her to emerge and evolve in her life's journey. Along with her partner, L. Roi Boyd lll, she travels to new destinations to enhance, and enrich her overall view of humanity in its many variations.

CONTRIBUTORS

Artful illustrations by Tina McGlynn - Cover Picture, page 4, page 12, page 15, page 35

Artful illustrations by Faithe Nordell Page 14, page 32

Artful illustration by Joel Fletcher - Page 20

Artful illustration by Susan Moncure - Page 33

Photographer Robert L. Sims III - Cover Picture, page 12, page 15

Photographer Frank Anderson - page 4, page 35, photographs of Matriarchs, photograph of Yemaja

Adinkra Symbols from http://www.adinkra.org/htmls/adinkra_index.htm

www.ingramcontent.com/pod-product-compliance
Lightning Source LLC
Chambersburg PA
CBHW061049090426
42740CB00002B/89